Gallimaufry

Antony Fawcus lives on a small farm behind Port Elliot, on the south coast of South Australia. He is widely travelled and has at various times been an aviator, a teacher and a tourism operator. Recent publications include *Written in Sand* (Ginninderra Press 2016), *The Ethiopian Afar and other poems* (Ginninderra Press 2015) and a chapbook called *Storms* (Ginninderra Press 2014).

Also by Antony Fawcus and published by Ginninderra Press
Storms (Pocket Poets)
The Ethiopian Afar
Written in Sand

Antony Fawcus
Gallimaufry

This book is dedicated to you, the unknown reader,
who may chance to idle by

Gallimaufry
ISBN 978 1 76041 450 4
Copyright © text Antony Fawcus 2017
Copyright © cover image Anna Fawcus 2015

First published 2017 by
GINNINDERRA PRESS
PO Box 3461 Port Adelaide 5015 Australia
www.ginninderrapress.com.au

Contents

The Mobile Phone	9
Night Ballet	10
Under the Gooseberry Bush	11
Hunted	13
A Halloween Surprise	16
Forgiveness	17
At the Still Point	18
Collateral Damage	19
Loss	20
Shore Leave	21
Temptation	23
Border Control	24
What it Takes	25
The Awakening	26
Navigating by the Stars	27
Infidelity	28
What Is This Moon?	29
The Haggis	30
The Fireworks of Delight	31
The Cowrie Shell	32
Bacchanalia	34
Music	35
Farewell	36
The Final Word	37
The Garden Door	38
Late for the Wedding	39
The Winter Fishing Fleet	40
Early Lambing	41
Late Autumn	42
The Commuter	43

Beyond the Oasis	44
The Sacrifice	46
Spellbinding	47
The Sneezing Schnauzer	48
At Morning Prayer	49
The Self-portrait	51
Caution	52
Dawn	53
A Requiem	54
The Moonlit Pool	56
For the Love of Words	57
Old-time Movies	61
The Lone Skier	62
Syria	63
Scrumpy	64
The Wounded Poet	65
Sydney Mardi Gras	66
Petrarch's Cat	67
I Fain Would Kiss	68
Cheers!	70
To Desdemona	71
The Changing Face of Beauty	72
How Beauty Fades	73
The Wind	74
Mimi	78
A Rose by Any Other Name	80
The Song Thrush	81
Define Yourself	84
The Chase	85
Digging Holes	86
The Plague	89
The Shadow	90

A Moment in Time	91
Kismet	93
Long Days I Languish	94
Night Flight	95
The Silence of the Stars	97
Toy Soldiers	98
Choices	99
The Spartan Nest	100
The Thrift Shop	101
Trust	102
Teagan Arrives	103
Protection	104
Teagan, Hashtag Poet	105
Squirrel Thought	106
A Snow Job	107
The Morris Dancer	109
The Rich Poet	110
The Semantics of Love	111
The Poor Poet	112

The Mobile Phone

A Shakespearean sonnet

A modern miss with all her wares displayed,
my darling has a svelte and slender frame,
she is so chic in skin-tight purple suede,
I fondle her in public without shame.
I often press her buttons to arouse
that soft electric glow that lights her dial.
She satisfies my urgent need to browse –
my thumbs caress her belly all the while,
but my compulsive texting leaves her flat,
her face goes blank just when I need her most,
I dread the warning light that tells me that
she'll be asleep before I've sent my post.
I feel so disconnected and alone,
recharging my beloved mobile phone.

Night Ballet

Beyond the bounds of day
is where the wild words play,
like dancers wearing daisies,
like puppies with the crazies,
like butterflies that swarm,
like flames to keep us warm,
like ocean breezes calm,
and love that does no harm.
Their ballet in the brain
inhabits nights alone.
Ephemeral as frost,
with sunrise they are lost.

Under the Gooseberry Bush

This stump with orange rump of Turkey Tail,
a fungoid fan that feeds on creviced skin,
sequestered by the spider's dewy veil,
hides a tale of secret life within.

For though the tree is dead, there still remain
fond memories of green and lithesome years
when branches stretched to shade a country lane,
caressed by summer's gift of gentle tears

distilled to droplets, hanging from each leaf,
a crystal canopy to shade from showers,
a sanctuary and shelter, underneath
this chestnut, with its candlesticks of flowers,

and here the throstle serenaded them,
a loving pair who caused the sun to shine
again. When Cupid smiled they did succumb
and, as two honeysuckles intertwine

in sweetness, they conceived unhallowed joy.
Next year the tree was felled by savage storms;
likewise the bastard child was dropped – a boy.
The speckle-breasted thrush returned to mourn

and on that wretched stump let fall a seed,
then, in his search for grubs, he drilled it in.
It prospered and grew thorns, lest common greed
should pluck its fruit, compounding mortal sin.

The boy set out, his origin to learn –
beneath this gooseberry bush, the whispered breath,
a foundling child, conceived in sinful squirm.
What rottenness is this that grows from death?

He gorged upon the hairy goosegog fruit
and kicked the Turkey Tail from off the stump.
He was a wicked child, a little brute,
and got his just desserts – a stomach pump.

He turned from bad to worse as years went by
I have to say his sins disgusted me.
His crimes resulted in a hue and cry
and now the gooseberry fool's in custody.

Hunted

Terza rima

As he approached the oracle
a vulture circled in the sky.
He quickly beached his coracle

and dragged it to the reeds nearby.
Why came this loathsome bird to feed?
Alas, he guessed the reason why.

He crossed the plain with little heed,
as, rock by rock, this barren land
tore blistered feet and made them bleed.

At last he left the scorching sand
to start the final craggy climb,
a journey leaving him unmanned

for he was running out of time,
and still the vulture circled round,
a grim reminder of his crime.

At length, he reached the higher ground
and turned his gaze across the sea
from whence he came while others drowned.

The vulture landed in a tree.
It held its grip with wrinkled claw
and eyed his heart malevolently.

Then, far below, upon the shore,
he spied another wicker craft
dragged up the beach, as his before,

by two dark shapes, one fore, one aft,
his nemesis, he was pursued,
with his death warrant autographed.

He grasped the rocks, his flight renewed,
and climbed again with fevered haste.
His safety lay in altitude.

For many weeks, these wraiths had chased
relentlessly to hunt him down,
and now at last they had the taste

of blood that stains the victor's gown –
that crimson guilt of mighty men
that flows to forge each kingly crown.

Above, to save him, lay the den
that held the jewel-encrusted key
(of which he learned by power of Zen)

to turn the lock and set him free.
He strove with his remaining breath,
in hope to reach this sanctuary

before the shades who sought his death
should gain more ground and close the gap,
and then pronounce their shibboleth,

those potent words, his soul to trap.
Beelzebub and Astaroth
have arts with which to weave and wrap

their lies within a monkish cloth
to seem like truth. Each sleight of tongue
corrupts, as does the soft-winged moth.

He battled on with burning lung
until at last he reached the place
of which the ancient seers had sung,

but there he found he'd lost the race.
There was no key absolving guilt,
and no escape from his disgrace.

The hope that, in his mind, he'd built
to finally escape the Fates,
dissolved as did the blood he'd spilt.

When faced head-on by desperate straits
he'd made the choice to save his skin
and saved himself by drowning mates.

Death now loomed, its hideous grin
the final price for his foul sin.

A Halloween Surprise

A rondeau

This Halloween, when children don disguise
to beg from me their treats, with wails and sighs,
and witch's hat and broom, and blacked out tooth,
put on to hide their innocence and youth,
I have in store for them a bleak surprise.

I shall, but in reverse, respond likewise,
removing my false teeth, to hear their cries
when they discover age holds horrid truth
this Halloween.

My hearing aids are off, their screaming dies!
My glasses shall no longer be my spies
to soften me towards their dreadful ruth.
Decrepitude is frightful, too, forsooth!
You'll shield your little monsters, if you're wise
this Halloween.

Forgiveness

A villanelle

Some people have that gift for giving things
but I do not. Abject apology
is, oh, so hard for me at times and stings

me into shame. I compensate with rings
and then chuck chocs and roses in for free.
Some people have that gift for giving things!

Some gifts are wasps; some, butterflies with wings.
The perfect choice, that hovers like a bee,
is, oh, so hard for me at times, and stings!

I have a friend with silver tones who sings
but, like a dog, I bark – you would agree.
Some people have that gift for giving things,

but I am hopeless and the stigma clings.
The perfect choice that's clarified, like ghee,
is, oh, so hard for me sometimes, and stings

and unkind, sharp rebukes my true love flings,
hit home. Her taunts annoy. They anger me!
Some people have that gift! Forgiving things
is, oh, so hard for me at times and stings.

At the Still Point

'At the still point…
there the dance is' – T.S. Eliot

Perfect balance
en pointe conceals
long years of pain
behind the smile

of those who stand on tips of toes
to seek beyond
the rainbow and its tears.

Collateral Damage

Blank verse

Who are the herdsmen in this wilding night
that gather up the straggled waywardness
of those who clothe their weak, subsistent selves
in shrouded veils of faded silken dreams?

How safe is walled defence against fell wraiths
whose howling makes the nightmares shift and stamp,
intent to tear them free from stable thought,
white-eyed with terror, baring foam-flecked teeth?

Who saddles them, these fearsome warhorse mounts
that carry fallen angels, poisoned breath
and hate? What drives the palpitating beat
of drums that thud in honour of a god

against the weak and frail, who crouch behind
thin walls of clay and wait, no place to go?
Apocalyptic horsemen ride once more
to raze the withered remnants. No recourse.

Loss

What have I lost today?
My keys, my faith, my way,
but you were born.

What lost I from the night?
My dreams and second sight,
devoured by dawn.

In time I'll lose my mind
and find my words unwind,
scattered and torn.

What if I lose my soul,
but keep my body whole?
Of self I'm shorn.

What if I lose my life
under the surgeon's knife?

*

Why, then I'm gone.

Shore Leave

A still night, a quiet night,
with humid, listless air,
frangipani fragrance,
moonlight's wanton stare.

Lazy fans swing slowly,
lifting up my prayer,
but God alone knows where.

A one-eyed beggar's squatting
on the fraying copra matting
near a broken rattan chair.

A cradled sampan's rocking,
its painted eyes are mocking,
and it's knocking,
like a toothless harbour whore,
kelp and mango slopping
at the restless, upright oar,

and sailors come ashore
to sample fruits like these,
exquisitely diseased.

The magenta mangosteen,
a short-lived tropic queen,
leather skinned but sweet within,
white-pulped flesh sucked from the stone,
juices dripping, putrid brown
to stain and mock the bridal gown

and deities forgotten
mid detritus that's rotting
upon the harbour shore,

and here the urchin children play,
whose searching eyes
alight today
upon an amputated doll,
a broken, pink-cheeked, plastic moll
with innocence surprised,
and arms outstretched
to flail the heavy-scented air
that's lifting up my moonlit prayer
to God alone knows where.

God alone knows where.

Temptation

A rondel

Pert nubile nubs of alabaster,
enchantment, and an elfin smile,
caught his eye – no denial.
A seaman courting sweet disaster,
he felt his vagrant heart beat faster
as she exercised her guile,
pert nubile nubs of alabaster,
enchantment, and an elfin smile.
From that day on and ever after,
he was imprisoned on her isle,
captured by her female wile.
She tenderly enslaved him with her
pert nubile nubs of alabaster,
enchantment, and an elfin smile.

Border Control

Thus I mused while pulling weeds
and planting seeds
in my exotic plot,
this Camelot.

Carefully tending those I love:
kiss-me-quick and Damask rose,
fuchsia and valerian,
favoured plants, invited in.

Another wave of migrants came,
an uninvited yellow bane,
an acid flower,
unwelcome, sour,

that broke my pre-set rules
with adventitious propagules,
invasive plant and uncontrolled.
My heart grew cold.

What it Takes

A rondeau redoublé

Strike on your drum with a boom and a brazenness,
striding out forcefully, stepping out merrily,
echoing confidence, displacing laziness,
singing most tunefully, jauntily, airily.

Make it more notable, beat it more scarily,
life can be changeable, fill it with craziness,
dance without fear like a grizzled old bear! Really
strike on your drum with a boom and a brazenness.

Life may be filled with a feeling of haziness,
making one miserable unnecessarily.
Snap out of lethargy! Leap up with wakefulness,
striding out forcefully, stepping out merrily,

giving a wave to the bystanders, cheerily
bellowing, 'Follow me! Celebrate zaniness!
It's not the garden variety!' – verily
echoing confidence. Displacing laziness,

make it more difficult, put away caginess,
leap on a bicycle, pedal most hairily,
drumming one-handedly, not minding shakiness,
singing most tunefully, jauntily, airily.

Do not be hesitant, never go warily,
celebrate crashes but learn when you make a mess.
Rise from the ashes – remember, not fearfully!
Show you have courage and resonate agelessness
…strike on your drum!

The Awakening

A Petrarchan sonnet

A single bird awakes to brightly sing
in silver as the sun begins to spill
its gold upon the sleeping daffodil;
such wealth to woo the breaking day and bring
from other waking birds a burgeoning
of joy, with sunlight creeping down the hill
to thaw the bones of patient kine and thrill
new lambs to life with cheerful twittering.
But I would miss the dawn to be with you
wrapped in my arms, with curtains drawn, held tight
against the light, lest it should steal our time
for further dalliance, to sip the dew
and taste again the pleasures of the night.
The censor cuts! It's time to end this rhyme!

Navigating by the Stars

Terza rima

When all is dark and I am feeling lost
my inner compass swings uncertainly
and paths I thought were sure once more are crossed.

It is at times like this, when I'm at sea,
in solitude I scan the night-time sky,
where signs in starlit patterns speak to me.

I search the Southern Cross to verify
my way. Though I've been here for thirty years
my origins still call as, with a sigh,

I recollect the Pole Star calmed my fear
before I chose to change my hemisphere.

Infidelity

A rondeau

Cuckoo! Cuckoo! Here comes the spring!
A sweet bird calls with words that wing
into my heart. She is a dear!
I am in love! She brings me cheer
and soon in unison we sing.

She flaunts a leg. My pants go ping
so I invest, and there's the sting!
My marriage nest is wrecked, I fear.
Cuckoo! Cuckoo!

But I enjoyed that little fling
that played my heart and broke a string,
A brief affair without a care
before she flew to nests elsewhere.
Oh what a tease! The sexy thing!
Cuckoo! Cuckoo!

What Is This Moon?

A villanelle

What is this moon, this fetid pool of light,
this alabaster shadow of disease
that frames the death mask of a pallid wight,

like swaying gibbet bones in anchored flight,
no longer subject to life's leprosies?
What is this moon, this fetid pool of light

that seeps across the clammy skin of night
through holes where worms have eaten through the frieze
that frames the death mask of a pallid wight?

Its yellow discharge oozes like a blight,
gangrenous on this pockmarked, rotting cheese.
What is this moon, this fetid pool of light

that hauls upon the tides, this satellite
that dares deflect our lives, our certainties?
Who framed the death mask of this pallid wight

that angles with his line; a parasite
eroding solid shores with shifting seas?
What is this moon, this fetid pool of light
that frames the death mask of a pallid wight?

The Haggis

Gloom in the rumen
while roamin' in the gloamin'
…haggis lies heavy.

The Fireworks of Delight

A Shakespearean sonnet

How huge the movement of the stars that span
the sky above our world, and yet they're still
uncomprehended by the eye of man,
more used to sparks from human fires that thrill
and flare but fail, like comets too soon spent.
Freed from the field of scars on satin skies
in one ecstatic shiver of descent,
their lurid tale shines brief before demise.
Though stars may fill the firmament of minds
their fire's too far away to make us burn.
It is your closer touch that gently finds
the constellation of desire I yearn.
Let others gaze at stars throughout the night,
while we ignite the fireworks of delight.

The Cowrie Shell

Free verse

When death is asked
to come before its time,
it takes a tithe.

We, the mourners who survive,
die by tenths inside,
and, into the deep
and empty void,
a well of sadness seeps.

Our surge of grief
rolls in waves ashore,
writing Kaori's song anew.

An echo of the life we knew
now fills the cowrie shell
that's thrown against the shore

and, if we hold it to our ear,
we shall hear
a resonance to fill the space
between our stars and hers,
an incandescent shimmering
to splash against the rampart
shoreline of our love.

Memories are maintained
to drive the drowning out,
with joy for what we shared.

The sadness lasts,
but she would wish with all her heart
that we be whole again,
to live our lives in full,
in thankfulness
for happy years we shared.

Bacchanalia

Anacreontic verses

Serve the oysters up again,
pop the cork on the champagne.

Ecstasy should never wait.
Seize the chance! It's getting late.

Come with me to bed tonight
just as we are getting tight.

Hum the 'Moonlight Serenade'
as your ankle is displayed.

When the pipes of Bacchus sound,
nothing then is out of bounds.

Music

Whence comes this love affair?
Is it in the womb,
the heartbeat measure of a mother's love,
that feeds and nurtures with each pulse of blood?
Or is it when we get our first guitar,
whose shapely waist
provides us with the taste
for more?
A lifetime lies ahead to hunger for.

Farewell

A pantoum sonnet

Our stars are dancing on the sea tonight
yet shudder at the sadness of farewell,
alive in this blue hour of shifting light.
I watch the way they ride the rising swell
yet shudder at the sadness of farewell.
Such sea-glass stars have twins set in the sky.
I watch the way they ride the rising swell
as we must surely do; my love and I.
Such sea-glass stars have twins set in the sky
that span the empty loneliness of space
as we must surely do, my love and I,
until we can, at length, again embrace.
Our stars are dancing on the sea tonight
alive in this blue hour of shifting light.

The Final Word

I searched the lexicon last night
to find the final word,
definitive, beyond dispute,
but 'zygote' was absurd.

The fusion of two cells or souls
defines the start of life.
It's only fission marks the end,
when atoms split in strife.

Then in another tome I found
my bank of words extended.
The zygote now gave up its claim
to be the word that ended.

It was, instead, a Zyrian.
He echoed wolves of old,
whose host destroyed Sennacharib
in cohorts, gleaming gold.

Imagine, though, a man of peace,
if that's not too absurd,
unprejudiced, espousing love…
a finer final word!

The Garden Door

His garden door of Chinese red's
unhinged. Not dead, for still
his ashes feed the lily bed.
I think they ever will.
His secret paths are now outgrown
by humble plants he loved, self-sown
by winds that lift a sacred moan.
Hong Shi enthrones his hill.

I shall recall the Hodmandod
with gumboots shod, his mind
in harmony with self and god,
a concept he defined
in terms of Nature. Still his soul
inhabits me and makes me whole.
When at his spring, I pledge my bowl,
consoled and re-aligned.

Late for the Wedding

The choirboys splash along the puddled lane.
In haste they race to church for they are late.
Its clock begins to chime just as they gain
the weathered steps beyond the blackthorn gate

where blossoms like confetti fly and swirl,
as if they need rehearse before the bells
ring out for joy, with peals of mirth, like girls.
They tease the blushing bride. Her stomach swells,

a fervid germination of desire,
for she is elemental, one with earth.
Pink buds unfurl upon the virgin flower
to celebrate the joy of coming birth.

The Druids buried eggs they daubed in red
to draw the life force from the dormant soil
to signify the drops the hymen bled;
an ancient rite that blessed the farmers' toil.

Pejorative, we label hers as sin,
but is it sin to love with all one's heart?
The seeds of love are deep ingrained within
the wounds, when Cupid hurls his deadly dart.

The Winter Fishing Fleet

A heroic sonnet

At anchor now, a jousting host of masts
slop-wallow as they slacken off their stays.
A watercolour sky, when sunlight casts
an aureole through mists to backlight bays
where bar-tailed godwits stand on jointed sticks,
in estuaries ablaze with winter's glow
and dunlins spear small shrimps on mudflat slicks
'mid shallows left by ebbing tidal flow,
but how this calm belies the banshee yell
of North Sea winds swept from the Russian steppe
when herring buss and doggers ride the swell.
These winter fishing fleets that strain and schlep
their laden nets of mack'rel, cod and skate
have weathered fearsome storms with mighty waves
when fishermen themselves are tossed as bait
for kraken monsters, deep in briny graves.
At times the bravest hearts may skip a beat,
but there are those at home who need to eat.

Early Lambing

A heroic sonnet

Rejoice, a new year comes, and with it, hope,
though snow with cold still numbs the silent Peaks
and spring's submerged beneath the crusted slope,
her gentle words too frozen yet to speak.
There is a crystal sharpness in the air,
a glint of sunlight, sent to vaporise
the tinge of frost on twisted branches, where
awaking catkins shake in warm surprise,
as if to greet the winter lamb that frisks
to save herself and shake away the cold.
Such joyfulness is unaware of risks,
but she'll be safe tonight, within the fold.
Whilst jagged granite outcrops can withstand
the cruel winter blasts that swirl around,
this premature arrival needs a hand
to weather winter storms on safer ground,
for in the face of howling upland gales,
too rash a breath of life declines and fails.

Late Autumn

Free verse

The woods are still,
the leaf a whispered fall
that comes to rest –
the last of all…
foreshadowing
the winter snow.

Beyond the fire,
a golden glow,
and wisps of smoke,
that wreathe the trees
in fading light
and reverie.

The Commuter

Blank verse

With forehead pressed against the cold, damp glass,
he gazed upon the scattered dots of sheep,
their woolly shapes appliquéd to the hill,
stitched up in time, as he went rattling past,
fixed on a destination foreordained,
and, deep in thought, he gazed upon the world,
the foreground just a blur as it flashed by,
but distances more clear, as patterned fields
gave up their cultured calm for wilderness.

At length he turned an inward eye upon
his fellow passengers within the train,
in cramped compartments, perched, with sightless stares
and wheels that ruled their minds in mute accord
with railroad clicks and clacks that measured time
on this, the eight-oh-four to Waterloo.

Like hens, their pecking order was assured,
defined by pinstriped suits and old school ties.
And then he thought of home and coddled eggs,
free range, of course, as young men ought to be.

How sad his wings were clipped at boarding schools
that taught conformity and etiquette.
The brokers' rooms were safe and beckoned him,
so with a sigh he opened up his case
to spread *The Times*, while folding up his dreams.

Beyond the Oasis

Free verse

Let me pack this poem
with things that cannot be spoken,
feelings too deep to feel,
too wide to embrace,

and too high to sustain
the struggling breath of inspiration.

Let me mourn the loss
of those things
that lie beyond my imagination;
the elusive, folded spaces of time.

Does a fragrance of roses linger in the vase,
and is this the gentle breeze
that kissed the cheeks of absent friends,
in memory of times now flown?

Is this the shade of darkness that defines the light,
the armour of outline
that cloaked shapes wear
to fend negative space
from their nakedness?

A shaft of coloured light
illuminates a galaxy
of dust specks;
an infinity
with shadowed edges,
and bloodstains on cold grey stone.

Does the flower arranger feel my presence
each time I revisit this church of my ancestors,
that is no longer there?

What is poetry,
but the filling of one space with another?

And what is this rush of wind,
the dreaded Ghibli
that obscures each page with sand,
making once more a desert of emptiness,
while stinging my eyes with grains of truth
beyond the oasis.

The Sacrifice

Where's my mate's dad, the man of war
I never saw,
who gave his life
in that great strife?

'The War to End All Wars', they said,
but he is dead
and still there's war,
just as before.

The old men said his sacrifice
was worth the price.
I think they lied,
but you decide.

Spellbinding

Should I, a poet, be berhymed to death,
as in the ancient days of spells confessed,
enchanted by the chants and thus confused
as rats, amazed in wheels of words, bemused?

Or should my verse be free of echo's chains,
reliant on my wit, or what remains
of it, as I decline and conjugate
my predicated words, most profligate

in flights of fancy, dancing on the page
like spells of necromancy when a mage,
wizened in his wizardry, makes sparks fly?
Such fireworks blaze in fierce display then die.

What artistry lies in this artifice?
Linguistic sophistry I would dismiss
for the emotion felt in simple words,
and the clear voice that's found in songs of birds.

The Sneezing Schnauzer

(with apologies to Dr Seuss)

I've read your *Fox in Socks*, sir.
He's a tongue-twisting blister
and my tongue's still twisted, mister,
but here's a tale of Teagan's schnauzer,
So pay attention, do sir, now, sir!
He's not a cat. He doesn't miaow, sir,
he won't chase string,
he's not a mouser.
If he could speak, he'd say bow wow, sir.
Sometimes he travels incognito
but in New York he's called Pablito.
Oh, Pablo! Pablo! Oh, Pab…lito!

A schnauzer's sneeze is full of fleas
But in the winter his fleas freeze.
Frozen fleas freeze schnauzer's noses.
Where do frozen sneezes flee to?
Where do freezing snow fleas go to?
Oh, Pablo! Pablo! poor Pab…lito

What a nasty sneeze you've got!
I think you've drowned a small mosquito
with your sneeze of rocket snot.

At Morning Prayer

Free verse

A shadowed wraith on weak arthritic limbs,
the old horse leaves his shelter-belt of trees
beneath a sickle moon.

From the still and patient night,
there breathes a whispered breeze
to beckon him,
as it has done before.

He slowly comes with measured tread,
to stand upon an earthen wall
above the pool reflecting him,
and, facing east, he waits.

His chestnut coat
by night bedewed,
his head and neck held low
as if in prayer,
and there, stock-still, he stands,

until the first sharp rays
break out above the hill
to bathe his ears in splendour,
then his back,
brazing him once more,
a burnished bronze,
fit for Bellerophon to ride
against the Chimera of day.

The shadows, mute, shrink back
aghast,
in reverential awe.

Still, this ancient horse stands still
as does the world and time,
his head now raised
to breathe a wisp of breath,
a soft grey incense
silvered by the dawn.

And then, to hail this newborn day,
there starts a joyful chorus,
the orison of birds.

The Self-portrait

This colour wash's a birthing on the blank,
at first an open sky of palest blue,
a background for the brushstrokes yet to come
as, given time, I gain a deeper hue.

Who is the artist with the sable hair
that's laden with the pigment of my life?
What colours will he choose to paint the tale?
What vibrancy to boldly paint the strife?

And will he turn the errors into clouds,
embellish them to make a flight of birds,
or add a wicker basket strung below,
in which to float beyond these barren words?

Caution

A Shakespearean sonnet

My heart has wandered weary miles at sea
and seeks to rest upon this foreign strand.
Although diaspora displaces me,
and circumstance has stamped me with the brand
of homelessness, alone and incomplete,
in last night's dock I felt the rising swell
of your strong pulse. It caused my heart to beat
with tantalising dreams I can't dispel.
But, after all the disappointments past,
I hesitate to bind myself to you,
for I have learned to fear the bait that's cast.
I see the glinting hook and taste the rue.
My mouth still bleeds though I escaped before,
so spin your line elsewhere. The wound is raw.

Dawn

Free Verse

Light filtered through the eucalypts
at dawn, a radiance divine,
renascent jewels to crown the air,
a shower of stars that came,
cascading through the leaves
to quench the night
with the first cool draught of day,
all else still dark.

I thought that sight to be
a foretaste of eternity.
Not age nor dotage
nor opacity
can close an inner eye,
etched with such a memory.

In the last grey fog of pain,
a softened halo seen
through mists of time,
will come back again
to lay the pallid smile
of Mnemosyne,
on death's pale lip,
in closure,
for that final flight alone,
the last leaf turned.

A Requiem

If you should chance to pass this way
one day when I am gone,
the pause you make will bring to life
the man who wrote this song.

Forever frugal with his love,
he locked it into words.
Oh, do not make the same mistake,
give yours away to birds.

Although they be ephemeral,
they sing with all their heart,
and other birds take up the song
soon after they depart.

For life is in the blossoming,
the wise let it unfold
without much thought for future wealth.
The present tense is gold.

And yet perhaps in reading me,
you'll find a common bond
with one who valued solitude
beside the moonlit pond.

The fact you paused from life awhile
to dip into this tome,
suggests the linking of two souls
in other ways alone.

Some words become immortal,
a lonely state at best,
so when you've read these, burn them
and let them lie at rest.

Then go out and live your life,
and free yourself from care.
You once were earth, again will be.
Enjoy your breath of air.

The Moonlit Pool

An octogram

My footprint formed a shallow bowl
at dead of night,
that trapped the moonlight's lucent soul
of silver bright.
Reflected in the rippled pool
a scythe of death, a dancing jewel
that beckoned like a barrow wight
at dead of night,

and thus the moonlit mirror stole
me from your sight.
I listened to the waves cajole
to seal my plight.
The crescent cut my heart away;
its beauty led my mind astray
in silver shards of fractured light
at dead of night.

For the Love of Words

Free verse

Do you love your words
in the heat of passion,
in the frenzy of lust,
in the cold moonlight,
in the close juxtaposition
of sound and echo
in the halls of memory,
or do your words just lie
in the caves of unwritten desire?

Do they dwell in still, small spaces,
the heartbeats of the firmament?

Are they your children,
innocent, playful, incongruous,
dressed in gingham frocks?
Do your words have buck teeth and pimples,
are they shy and nervous,
do they shine through tears?

Are your words
all fingers and thumbs,
staccato stabs at utterance
tapped out on keys,
unlocking a new language with acrimonious brevity
that profanely screams its love to God. Oh, my…!
and lolls and rolls on floors in laughter,
as idle youths will do?

Are they born in wealth and beauty,
or do they struggle, as beggars on the street?
In need of love,
either way.

Are they words of courtly love, outpourings
of medieval beauty and verbal foreplay,
or do they stammer like a palpitating heart
that's long on passion, short on art?

Are they blunt
with the Saxon brevity of fuck and cunt,
or is theirs
the long lascivious flow of copulation?

Do they talk and pray
or stalk and prey?

Do they drive you to despair,
a firefly hunt in forest gloaming,
rustling through an alliteration of leaves
upon the forest floor,
leaves that conceal a still hiss of sibilance?
Do they flicker briefly with a forked tongue,
or speak their truth bravely?

Do they fight one another,
ungainly elephants that trample grass,
or do they wallow like thesaurus wrecks,
drowning in seas of dead language,
dragged down by the barnacles and bladderwrack
of scholarship?

Or do they traipse through meadows,
carefree and blithe,
inhaling simplicity and toxic air?

Are your words robust,
driving chariots of fire across the sky
to stir new life
from the crustiness
of this old and wrinkled world?

Are they siren words to coax seafarers,
or siren words, wailing
as they cut through traffic
raucously,
racing to hospital
with your cold hands grasping
against the ebb tide of death?

Do they conjugate and sing,
stretch the syntax of the known
to seek new fields in which to lie
watching leaves spin, and wondering why
such life of pulsing green
should turn vermilion and scream
against the storm,

then drift down
to rest
in peace,

freed from the seething ferment
of the mind?

Old-time Movies

Free verse

Celluloid see-throughs
reeling in our fantasies
like trout on the fly.

We sit there gormless,
hearing the whirring machine,
then it slips the spool.

All now unravels,
dreams in swirls upon the floor
as the lights go out.

The Lone Skier

Blank verse

The pine trees stand upon the mountainside,
aloof in their encrusted ermine robes,
each crystal gem a burden, weighs them down,
no muffled sound escapes. A stillness reigns
as if the world had stopped in wonderment,
the silence deep and pure, a pause in time,
until a skier comes, hunched down and poised,
such balanced grace and ease, a rhapsody
of rhythmic turns. Each slalom sprays the snow
from side to side like wings intent to soar,
a piste-bound swan that yearns release in flight
but then sinks back again. The sound subsides
and trees, a background then, assert themselves
once more, to rule this frozen citadel,
erect and proud, as they withstand the cold
and wait, in patient certitude, for spring.

Syria

A triolet

Because of weapons friends supplied,
this war's dragged on for five long years,
and countless innocents have died
because of weapons friends supplied.
The allies rage on either side;
such waste of life, so many tears.
Because of weapons friends supplied,
this war's dragged on for five long years.

Scrumpy

A pantoum

As last leaves fall, old limbs know winter's near.
A mist creeps in like yellow mustard gas,
a rottenness of apples fills the air,
and sleepy wasps are in the orchard grass.

A mist creeps in like yellow mustard gas
while drinking in the sun's last golden ray,
and sleepy wasps are in the orchard grass,
too drugged by drunkenness to crawl away.

While drinking, in the sun's last golden ray,
the pickers quaff their pints and pity Tom,
too drugged by drunkenness to crawl away,
awash with scrumpy now the harvest's done.

The pickers quaff their pints and pity Tom,
a rottenness of apples fills the air,
awash with scrumpy, now the harvest's done.
As last leaves fall, old limbs know winter's near.

The Wounded Poet

Let lightning strike and sear this pointless page
with voltages extreme and cyclone rage.
Oh, storm of blinding, cursèd words, rampage,

be free! – but pierce my heart before you fly.
Let blood illuminate this parchment lie
of mediocre musings, ere I die –

or should I bind the wound with woven thought,
till a cicatrix is formed by this clot?
My mind's anaemic, drained, and I'm distraught.

Again the scar will heal, but still I scrawl,
despite the certain fate that must befall
echoed raven words – never more banal.

Sydney Mardi Gras

A Shakespearean sonnet

I'm done with poesy, and mooncalf dreams,
for words will not suffice to 'scribe my Pat.
His capital makes him a Queen of queens,
though 'tis his fundament I'm looking at.
I must unhook my pretty curlicues
to tear apart the phrases of the moon
and ease them up the jacksie of my muse,
the while imagining how he might swoon.
Sweet iambs to the slaughter! All must go!
Dispel atrocious trochees from my thoughts!
Despondent that my spondee's far too slow
For Pat, who spurns me! 'Strewth, I'm out of sorts!
It's back to earth, and sodding misery
for one who thought that life was poetry.

Petrarch's Cat

A Petrarchan sonnet

Perhaps it's true that Petrarch owned a cat,
embalmed with care, and placed behind a glass,
though tourists think it somewhat second-class,
remarking it is bald as any rat,
a cat without a name, and somewhat tat.
Research suggests the facts are rather sparse;
contortions of the truth themselves surpass.
He never wrote about this acrobat!
So why devise deceits like this with guile?
Of course – it fascinates the tourist horde,
not versed, as we, in literary style.
No doubt the sonnets would have left them bored,
expecting more. It's hard to reconcile
the cash with truth when touting bards abroad.

I Fain Would Kiss

A sonnet sequence

I fain would kiss the alabaster cheek
of one with smiles of pearl and golden mane,
whose sapphire eyes hold hidden depths that speak
of ruby lips to drive a man insane.
The petals of a summer rose unfurling,
sublimely redolent of your perfume,
are soon full-blown, their faded petals swirling
in spindrift down, to rest on young love's tomb.
Yet you, my love, are not a china doll,
nor will your beauty fade when summer's passed.
There is no metaphor that can enthral
like your warm loveliness. It will outlast
the fragile toys of childhood and the rose;
compared with you, these things are barely prose.

Compared with you, these things are barely prose,
for you, my love, are far beyond compare.
My pen is dry. The verse that sometimes flows
in crystal streams, now eddies in despair.
As though migrating geese, my words have flown.
I feel the pinch of frost, for winter's come,
and when the snow falls soft, I'll be alone
with thoughts of you, my love – or else undone.
Yet, should you choose to save me from this fate,
the very air you breathe would cause a thaw
to bring the spring again into my gait,
for saffron crocuses are here once more.
Bold spring begets such stigmas of desire!
The thought of us alone sets me on fire.

The thought of us alone sets me on fire,
and from the ashes of despair behold
a phoenix, risen from the solar pyre,
Apollo's face on earth, of burnished gold.
Were I indeed immortal, like the gods,
omnipotent enough to gain your hand,
I would be sure to win against the odds,
and join with you – our love the ampersand.
But I am just an ordinary man
who loves you more than I can rightly tell,
with all my aching heart, as best I can,
tongue-tied and lost for words – consigned to hell.
My love for you gives strength, though knees are weak!
I fain would kiss your alabaster cheek.

Cheers!

A Shakespearean sonnet

If I should speak of love in sonnet form,
then let it be in terms not often heard,
devoid of moons and swoons and Hallmark corn.
Such soppy rhymes define one as a nerd.
Nor let it be of spring and rising sap,
nor roses with their scent and pricking thorns.
These nature notes are just a load of crap,
or compost – which is bull bereft of horns.
Instead of love, instinctive, entered blindly,
in which man shakes his spear in carnal lust,
let's talk of love that makes us treat man kindly.
Imperative! A better kind of must!
So love your fellow man and with him dine!
A toast to friendship! Raise a glass of wine!

To Desdemona

A Spenserian sonnet

Such beauty, Desdemona, graces thee
as mermaids in the ocean yearn to own.
Didst steal it from the sirens of the sea?
Didst sea nymphs look to thee and gently moan,
distraught that Neptune gave thee pearls on loan
to frame so sweet a smile, as might beguile
the richest king, to share with thee his throne?
In others, beauty fades and turns to bile,
but age matures and deepens thine, and while
love's ravages on others takes its toll,
thou grow'st more fair, as they must reconcile
themselves to subterfuge, to gain their goal.
Though life be brief, thy looks maintain the truth
that loving me prolongs thy time of youth.

The Changing Face of Beauty

A Petrarchan sonnet

How beauty rues the compromise of years,
confessing itself lost as days go by.
It's lifted by a breeze; a gentle sigh,
as autumn claims its due in misted tears.
The vespers' bell rings out to echo fears
that draw us to confess our lives awry,
when youth led us to think we'd rather die
than lose those looks, the envy of our peers.
But now we know, as we go hand in hand,
that what we took for beauty was a fake,
inspired to satisfy Dame Nature's needs.
A truer beauty dwells within the band
of plighted troth, and wedding oaths we make.
Our love is measured not in looks, but deeds.

How Beauty Fades

A Shakespearean sonnet

How beauty fades! It's gone within the hour,
virginity unfurled – once tasted – lost.
Such pleasures of the night, my sweet moonflower,
confer their nectared sweetness at a cost.
Pale beauty is a trap to lure the male,
inflate desire, and set the heart aflame
with burning lust, for nature must not fail.
As petals fall, seeds swell and lay their claim
as heart-throbs of another sort eclipse
the moonshine subterfuge of outer show.
The urge of motherhood conceives small lips
to suckle, and bring forth an inner glow.
Your beauty's reason is to give new life;
for this I love you all the more, dear wife.

The Wind

A creation myth

On this, the harvest feast,
we gather round the fire,
our stomachs warm
and full of beans,
and wait.

At last the tribal elders come
and take their place within the ring.
They shift and slightly fart,
as old men do.
The youngsters grin.

Then all is quiet.

The Whisperer now begins,
slow at first, in measured tones,
his eyes raised to the trees,
their tiny shift of leaves,
and wisp of campfire smoke
spiralling
towards the gloaming eventide.

'It was not always thus,' he said,
and so the tale began.
'In distant days, before the birth of man,
elemental forces ruled this world and warred.
Chubasco most was feared,
for he was invisible
in his woven cloak of air.

His sudden gusts
came unawares
to snuff the fire
and raise the sands in regiments
to swamp his foes.

A suffocating silence then ensued
as he skimmed across the spume,
to draw a deeper breath.

The skies grew dark and glowering
and from the depths of silence came a rumbling roar
as back he came,
astride the storm,
spitting tongues of fire
to assail the shore
with landlash surf
whipped by his lust,
as he rode in upon the swell.

He drove her towering waves ashore
with such ferocity that they came as one
vast curl of such immensity
it blocked the sun,

and with his claws he dragged the sea
across the wrinkled skin
of ancient earth
and gouged ravines,
and raised rock-piled mountains up
till mighty rivers bled.

At length the gentle sky stepped in
with tears
and begged for clemency.
Chubasco saw the reddened rim around her eye
and was ashamed.

The sun sank low, in sorrow, to the sea,
stretched out to calm her brow,
and smooth her silken skin.

The wind abated,
shrank back to nothingness
and hid.'

The old man paused, and then went on:

'Today he rustles leaves
and curls his fingers round our campfire smoke
but he is contained.
His fire is now held captive
in the bellies of wise old men,
whose stomachs churn
and sometimes let slip a breath of him.'

And having spoken thus,
The Whisperer turned
to face the youngsters
and…
with a twinkle in his eye,
let go a mighty breaking wind.

Mimi

Free verse

Flickering flames make cave art dance,
Illuminating lore,
Mimis, rock sprites,
dreaming
a tracery of song lines
thinly drawn
in umbers, yellow ochre,
and siennas, burnt and raw.

The songs within them hidden,
till understanding flames
the angles of their games,
and men commune,
connected,
harmonic
with their lore.

Imperilled
if we douse the flame,
and shut the Mimi out,
for darkness then will spread
like deadly wildfire smoke.

With all our dreams extinguished
the Mimis, with a sigh,
will hide in fissured rock again
and wait
till by and by,
the elongated truth of things
emerges, renascent,
in bones,
and aspirations,
strewn on the desert strand.

New men may come,
– some future age –
to learn and carefully draw
the wisdom that lies within
the teaching of those scattered bones
upon the desert shore,

…and with a sharper acumen
heed the beckoning of Mimi men,
fragile friends,
once more.

A Rose by Any Other Name

Free verse

I am upon a trellis bound,
pinned to the southern wall
by wayward limbs
and tragic chance;
a fiery dragon's prey,

unless the tales of old be true
and, pricking on the verdant plain,
a Redcrosse knight
with shield and sword
may chance to canter by, again.

Each day, in hope, I stretch my arms
and drink the dew of dawn,
while starstruck daisies gaze at me,
captive and forlorn.

But if, perchance, I rescued be,
in time, I will unfurl
a blushing glow
most maidenly
of damask
and of pearl.

The knight that sweeps me up, away,
may think me his, withal,
but soon will find,
if care he scorns,
that he is pricked,
and then will learn
that maidens may have thorns.

The Song Thrush

A ballad

Maeve lightly tripped across the moor
as lark song filled the air,
a liquid spill of sunlit notes
to match her golden hair.

She skirted bogs of asphodel
to keep her lover's tryst,
where grasses wave their purple heads,
as soft as Achill mist.

Brown waters of a mountain stream
swirled past her, over scree,
so lithe, alive with dragonflies
and elfin mystery.

Its laughter matched the love that surged
in her expectant breast,
as up the mountainside she climbed
the path to Croaghaun's crest,

for there before the day was done,
'mongst lilac bells of ling,
she'd pledge her life to her true love,
and with the selkies sing.

But, as she gazed upon the moor,
a swirling wisp of cloud
began to cloak familiar rocks
beneath its cotton shroud.

Expecting her true love to come
to wrap her in his arms,
she kept her watch on Croaghaun's crag
suppressing growing qualms.

At length she left the meeting place
to search for her *leannán*.
As daylight faded into gloom,
her hopes sank with the sun.

Then Sith, the grey-winged faerie child
with eyes of em'rald green,
began a song whose words beguiled
young Maeve, the sweet colleen.

With spells she wove a silken thread
of lies to lead astray,
and feigned the curlew's plaintive cry
to lure Maeve from the way.

In frantic search she tripped and fell
into a stagnant pool,
and sank beneath the drowned moonlight;
a ghoulish death and cruel.

At dawn upon the keening wind,
A white-tailed eagle flew
And spied a glint of gold upon
The silver veil of dew.

He swooped and took her in his claws,
in lands of youth to dwell,
where she became the mavis bird
a song thrush, philomel.

Now, in the spring, the mavis bird
nests in a rowan tree
with feathered leaves and berries red;
the bane of false faerie.

Define Yourself

A rondeau redoublé

Define yourself within your warring thought;
the youthful mind, a swirling sea of dreams,
relentless tides, afloat with flotsam, fraught
with possibility. Excitement screams!
The treasure trove, when we set out, all seems
obtainable, before put down as nought
by practicality, whose sneer exclaims,
'Define yourself within your warring thought.'
In turbid waters, like an aquanaut,
we search beneath the surface smithereens
of fractured light and ripple waves that caught
the youthful mind, a swirling sea of dreams.
Thus, floundering, we drown in ocean streams,
yet strive once more to board the idle yacht,
to ride the jealous wind that whips and creams
relentless tides, afloat with flotsam, fraught
with memories aplenty, overbought
in times of youth. Again this treasure gleams,
now washed ashore for doting eyes to sort
with possibility. Excitement screams
with new perspective. Wisdom now redeems
those things we pawned. Don't sell yourselves too short!
If wise, you'll swim with dolphins, not sardines
exchanging oil-filled cans for life. Cavort!
Define yourself!

The Chase

Paw raised and pricked-up ear,
stock still, your hackles rise,
pointing the scent of fear
sparks enflame your eyes,
a spring unsprung you leap, a lithesome hare the prize.

Such urgency unleashed!
Straining, you give chase,
impressionist pastiche,
as two bodies race,
with synchrony of heartbeat drumming out the pace.

Survival is his spur,
instinct drives him on,
his brownness just a blur,
and then he's gone.
With feigned disinterest now, to other scents you're drawn.

Digging Holes

Free verse

For a child
anything is possible

One day I began to dig a hole
to the centre of the earth
and out on the underside

It was a serious business
and occupied all my attention
for more than an hour

I scrabbled dirt
and dislodged hindrances
with perseverance
and fingers

I discovered gems
that I thought at first were stones
until I looked more closely

an earthworm, half wriggling
half stuck in clay
and the damp smell
of new turned earth
and leaves

It was a great undertaking
an important journey
beyond the understanding of adults
who only saw me play

After a while my hole was deep enough
to curl up inside and hide

a secret place
and so I covered it
before I was called for tea

It felt good to have a place
In which to curl
underneath the ground
alone
with just the dampness of the soil
a muffled sound of heartbeat
and the random song of birds

In later years
I dug no more
and stones were only stones
but I still dreamed
of how life might be upside down

and now I know

life is good
with time allowed
for digging holes
and planting seeds in them
that others, too, might grow

sometimes in my digging though
I wonder if
I might be more the right way up
at home

before, once more
I'm silent
deaf to the sound of heartbeat
and the random song of birds

The Plague

A paradelle

On silent wing,
on silent wing,
the sickness came,
the sickness came,
on silent wing. The reaper smiled,
the sickness came, and kissed each child.

Goodnight, it breathed
goodnight. It breathed,
and each child slept,
and each child slept.
It breathed goodnight and mothers wept.
Each child sneezed and then he slept.

But echoes stay,
but echoes stay
in nursery rhyme,
in nursery rhyme.
We may forget, but echoes stay
in nursery rhyme when children play.

The sickness came, and kissed each child.
On silent wing, the reaper smiled.
We may forget, but echoes stay
in nursery rhymes when children play.
It breathed goodnight and mothers wept.
Each child sneezed and then he slept.

The Shadow

Free verse

I shall arise and take me from the shadows of the night,
cast them off to start upon my day,
but one pleads miserably to stay
and I have not the heart
to shake him away.

He clings to my ankles beseechingly
and claims me for his own.

How long and thin he seems,
so undernourished,
and in my care he wanes.
By noon, the zenith of my life,
I'm glad to shake him off.
Be rid of him!

But no!
He lies beneath my feet
waiting patiently
to take the ascendancy
and lengthen once again
and blacker grow
as time goes by

How stretched I feel in this
the thinness of the day
as he pulls me into night again,
scythe in hand,
another victim
for his land.

A Moment in Time

Free verse

Should I step back in time today?
The museum bids me lose myself
in shadows of the past.
There is a dusty stillness there
of transient immortality.

Or should I sample celluloid reality,
a strange fiction of flickering lights,
animating visions of not yet,
and things that may not come?

Or shall I, perhaps, stay here,
and now,
in the sunshine,

and listen to the birds sing,
and breathe the scent of violets,
and watch the squirrels run

like jagged moments of dragonflies
in random dance;
stopping and starting,
as do the water boatmen

who pull and push their life along
a frail meniscus,
in the shade of lilies,
near drowning on the pond,

defying the bombardment of city sounds,

Or close my eyes
and feel
the breath of wind
that stirs the blossom trees?

An insect on a petal
floats gently down;
a vision of eternity,
falling out of time.

Kismet

A villanelle

I can't forget that villa – Nell,
that shagpile carpet where we lay,
where kismet cast its cruel spell,

the open fire, its glow, its smell,
spring late that year, still cold in May,
I can't forget that villa – Nell,

those dull explosions as bombs fell,
the shattered limbs and disarray
where kismet cast its cruel spell,

the charnel house of Dante's hell,
the pall of smoke that choked the day,
I can't forget that villa – Nell,

the jagged wound, the oozing well
of lifeblood spilled, to my dismay,
where kismet cast its cruel spell.

My life became a broken shell,
as in my arms you slipped away.
I can't forget that villa – Nell,
where kismet cast its cruel spell.

Long Days I Languish

A Petrarchan sonnet

Long days I languish in my prison cell.
Each dawn, a single ray begins its crawl,
to scribe the sloth of time upon my wall.
Its spotlit sparks of dust define my hell,
like will-o'-wisps in fields of asphodel,
whose sallow petals mock the yellow pall
of lily-livered mists, where shadows crawl,
creating ghosts I've grown to know too well.

Though I have built this prison in my mind,
I cannot quash that lonely ray of hope,
a luminant erosion of self-doubt
and thoughts of Styx. Tap-tapping like the blind,
toward this fulgent light I grope, and grope
beyond the walls I built to keep it out.

Night Flight

Two-thirds the speed of sound and six miles high
and yet it seems we're stationary in flight,
as slow we gallop through the darkling sky,
our hooves on cobblestones this turbid night.

Soft traceries of orange faintly glow,
suggesting warmth and shelter found within,
like tatters of mantilla lace that flow
to veil protruding bones and lambent skin.

Dark spectres hide the Zamboangan coast;
a puppet show of broken clouds that drift
across the basalt sea, each small grey ghost
deceiving those who take the graveyard shift.

And, poised on high, a hemisphere recedes,
a tilted bowl of rice for starving men,
whose polished grains of fractured moonlight feed
such minds as seek the nourishment of Zen.

Her twin becomes a silver boat confined
upon our wing, a crescent blur in form.
It holds its pace with us, as though inclined
to steal a ride towards the nascent dawn.

Illumination spreads across the land,
a phosphorescent manna for mankind,
a speckled shoal of fish, a sleight of hand,
that tempts a fishing fleet to drop behind.

I idly watch them slide, in retrograde,
as though impelled towards a vortex, deep
beneath the sea, where fabled mermaids played
sweet songs to lull such fishermen to sleep.

Our unrelenting tumult, in full swing,
impels us south to greet our manatees.
Meanwhile the mirrored moon drifts down our wing
and sails into the burnished, metal seas.

As our diurnal sphere shakes off the night,
impatiently new horses start to neigh.
Apollo's coach will soon begin its flight,
to shine a searing light on this new day.

The Silence of the Stars

A Petrarchan sonnet

The silence of the stars resounds with song,
a simple cadence heard in solitude
when every sense is focussed on the mood.
For, if the mind is still, and hearing strong,
a harmony's released, and we belong.
Internal resonance is gently cued
that strikes sweet chords of simple gratitude,
and sweeps away all jarring thoughts and wrong.
When traffic and the blare of city din
discordantly bombard us with their noise,
we rush from past to future without pause,
and do not hear the whispered voice within,
that softly speaks of peace and present joys.
Such human needs, mankind too oft ignores.

Toy Soldiers

A minute poem

I wonder if inside he cried
as my men died,
all killed in fun
with my big gun.

My soldiers on the window ledge
were on the edge,
no chance in hell
as each man fell.

His war the same, with stench and fear.
Did he despair
as he watched me
dispatch with glee?

Choices

A pantoum

Some signs suggest my choices lie elsewhere
in my eternal search for happiness,
as ego seeks for pleasure here and there,
and sometimes I get lost, I must confess.

In my eternal search for happiness
base lust and greed divert me, as does ire,
and sometimes I get lost, I must confess,
when roaming tempting highways of desire.

Base lust and greed divert me, as does ire,
while love eludes me. What a state I'm in
when roaming tempting highways of desire –
Although I know the answer lies within.

While love eludes me, what a state I'm in
as ego seeks for pleasure here and there.
Although I know the answer lies within,
some signs suggest my choices lie elsewhere.

The Spartan Nest

A Petrarchan sonnet

The Spartan nest is made of stick and thorn,
whose comfortless protection rears a bird
of prey, with strength respected and abhorred,
who strikes with steel and treats all prayers with scorn.
Some softer nests swing in the lambent corn,
and sway with ease on breezes lightly stirred
to rock their baby buntings, undeterred
by talons that would tear the newly born.
A loving hand upon the Spartan nest
might intercept the harshness of this law
that's writ in nature – that the weak shall fail.
The wounds upon such loving hands attest
attempts to alter nature have their flaw;
the bandaged hand of succour is impaled.

The Thrift Shop

Blank verse

Not far beyond the intersecting life
of 1st and 23rd, I paused awhile,
my shoulders hunched with cold, and then walked in
where Venus lay, embroidered on a seat,

beneath a reproduction, framed in gilt,
The Carmen Dolorosa of Seville,
whose salt damp tears had run and spoiled her robe.
The ticket with her price was turned in shame.

Among the dresses loosely slung on racks,
were jet set sequined eyes of beaded gowns
that glittered with svelte shapes of former days,
the bric-a-brac of long forgotten lives,

and there beside Stravinsky's *Rite of Spring*,
two onyx ducks at loggerheads, support
some hidebound books of Alexandrine verse
unsure which way to lean, a Morton's fork

beside a somewhat tarnished silver spoon.
A glint behind the glass then caught my eye;
a set of crystal goblets missing one –
the shattered truth of finite usefulness.

I stooped and thumbed a dollar from my roll,
to purchase Whitman's sighing *Leaves of Grass*,
before returning home the way I came,
with jumbled thoughts, and hopes, and hidden fears.

Trust

How small this hand,
how great the trust
that lies between our years.

With her small grip,
just one day old,
she crushes latent fears.

Six dozen springs
have now slipped by
since my lined hand was small,

and grasping for
infinity;
a time that's held in thrall.

There may be joy,
there may be woe,
but lies between the years

will not be told
to break this trust
that crushes hidden fears.

Teagan Arrives

A clerihew

Teagan Skye Lowry,
a poet, a priori,
has been born, is extant,
and is inclined to rant.

Protection

A *parapluie*
says phooey
to the rain

An umbrella
will dispel a
cloud above

A parasol
can forestall
the sunburn pain

But a bonnet
is a sonnet
scrawled with love

Teagan, Hashtag Poet

Between the Bronx and Bowery,
there lies a little Lowry

curled in fluid amniotic,
she'll soon be aeronautic.

A sudden surge will seize her,
she'll catch a wave to please her,

and come headfirst – chitter-chattin'
into central East Manhattan.

If you've got a bugle, blow it
to herald Teagan, hashtag poet.

Squirrel Thought

In Central Park
my squirrel thoughts
leap from tree to tree,

their zigzag race
releasing snow
upon a crocus sea;

a sudden pause,
a question mark,
as they look down at me.

It's then I strain
upon the leash,
yearning to be free,

but as I bark
they twitch their tails,
chitter repartee,

…then flee!

A Snow Job

Free verse

Soft
the snowflakes fall
from swirling skies;

a silent drift
that muffles
human margins;

a deadly flutter
that numbs the raw
of snow-grit
homeless heaps.

Listen!

Can you hear
the crunch
of frozen sidewalk smut
beneath that traffic noise
and siren scream?

I do not lie –
I need your money for the ice!
Rainbows
glisten in the sun
as it grows crystal cold.

Then comes the thaw,
and whirring snowplough brush
to sweep away
the residue of sidewalk slush,
assaulting grime
with tears.

The Morris Dancer

A pantygynt

What is this form, this pantygynt
who dances to the bells?
Two hundred miles was quite a stint –
all rivals he dispels!

> This Morris man's a dancer bold,
> (in wayside pubs the story's told)
> from Orpington, across the Wold,

Through Cotswold hills and dells

he danced six days in '81
(some years ago, I see!),
a hero's feat, when said and done;
immortal history!

> With sticks and hankies, the full kit
> he twirled and sang and was a hit
> while raising money – quite a bit!

He danced for charity.

E'en now one hears the music play
that echoes down the years.
He is the Piper's son, they say,
that calmed the Hamelin burghers' fears.

> No doubt the children followed him,
> entranced to see this dancing whim
> of our dear friend, the poet, Jim

who taps away our cares!

The Rich Poet

A rondeau redoublé variation

Each time he writes, the words declare him rich;
they represent a wealth beyond his dreams.
The straw he spins becomes a golden stitch
that sews his truth into each poem's seams.

His symphony of words explores extremes;
his voice is like a flute with perfect pitch;
his score is full of contrapuntal themes.
Each time he writes, the words declare him rich.

When rhyme and rhythm run without a hitch,
his freshly minted words are banked in reams.
Accounts are balanced with his quill's soft scritch;
they represent a wealth beyond his dreams.

Though wild the harvest tics may be, it seems
the scratch of pen on paper calms his itch.
He forages through thoughts and from them gleans.
The straw he spins becomes a golden stitch.

Some nights, he flagellates – his pen a switch
that tortures him with choices, till he screams
a necromancer's curse upon the witch
that sews his truth into each poem's seams.

She stirs the cauldron of his seething mind
with incantations to produce a charm
that weaves a cloth of gold for all mankind.
Such fantasies of fame act like a balm
each time he writes!

The Semantics of Love

A Shakespearean sonnet

The terms are strange we use to speak of love.
We say we fall in love, as if in sin,
but true love lifts, so let us rise above
ourselves, to find that higher place within.
In making love, we do not love create,
for love is more than urgent grunt and thrust.
In higher animals the urge to mate
transcends mere instinct, satisfying lust.
They say that Cupid's dart, unerring, finds
and pierces hearts. If that is true, we're dead.
True love is built more slowly in the minds
of lovers as they share their lives ahead.
The heart's a circulation pump – not more.
It is my head that leads me to adore.

The Poor Poet

An epitaph

Here rest the bones of penniless Peter,
whose body of poems died from lack of meter.
This ghosted credit indebts the poet;
both body and bones lie buried below it.

www.ingramcontent.com/pod-product-compliance
Lightning Source LLC
Chambersburg PA
CBHW070929080526
44589CB00013B/1448